AN ALBUM OF
WOMEN
IN
AMERICAN HISTORY

AN ALBUM OF
WOMEN
IN
AMERICAN HISTORY

CLAIRE R. & LEONARD W. INGRAHAM

FRANKLIN WATTS | NEW YORK | LONDON

Frontispiece: Marching in Washington, D.C., in 1913 to get the vote. The Capitol is in the background.

Cover design by Nick Krenitsky

Library of Congress Cataloging in Publication Data

Ingraham, Claire.
    An album of women in American history.

    (Picture albums)
    SUMMARY: Includes brief sketches of prominent American women and discusses the contribution of women throughout United States history emphasizing their struggles for equality.

    Bibliography: p.
    1. Women in the United States — History — Juvenile literature. [1. Women in the United States — History] I. Ingraham, Leonard W., joint author. II. Title.
HQ1410.15   301.41'2'0973   72-6138
ISBN 0-531-01515-7

CONTENTS

AN ALBUM OF
WOMEN
IN
AMERICAN HISTORY

INTRODUCTION

To the women who are part of what is commonly called "women's liberation," words are important. A quick look at a dictionary reveals why these women feel that such basic things as the meanings of words must be reexamined. For example, according to one dictionary definition, a woman is "a female human being (distinguished from male)," adding a "female person who cleans house, cooks, etc." In another part of the dictionary can be found the statement "LADY formerly implied family or social position, but is now used conventionally for any woman (esp. as a courteous term for one engaged in menial tasks)." It is no wonder that many women throughout history have felt "put down."

What is meant by "feminine"? In looking up all the words relating to females, it is not until we find the entry "feminism" that we begin to feel the winds of change. For "feminism" is defined as: "the doctrine advocating social and political rights of *women equal to men*." At last we can see the fact that women are not satisfied with dependence upon men, with inferior status, and that they are doing something about it.

This book will concern itself with those women in the history of the United States—from the earliest days of the Indian women, the colonial women, women during the western colonization, women of the Civil War period and the suffrage movement, and women during the two World Wars and up to the present liberation movement—who have chosen to speak up and to take an active role in society.

Women's liberationists all over the United States march on August 26, 1971, to demand equality. These were a few of the thousands who demonstrated in New York City on that day, the fifty-first anniversary of women's suffrage.

1

THE FIRST
WOMEN IN
AMERICA

Indian Women

Indian women joined their men to greet the early explorers. Though tribal customs and cultures differed, Indian women generally occupied a central position among their people. Some of them exercised a great deal of authority and received a large amount of respect. They often served as advisers to the men, in addition to looking after their own husbands and children and caring for the sick and infirm.

Busy from morning to night, Indian women reared their families, carried heavy loads, planted maize (Indian corn), cooked meals, and made clothing, which often required working with heavy leather and animal skins.

Whereas Indian women helped their men, often they were highly respectful of and even subservient to the men of the tribe, who were known as "the braves." The men, the hunters and fighters of the tribe, provided their families with food and with protection from the settlers, whom they came to regard as invaders.

The English colonists at Fort Raleigh on Roanoke Island, Virginia (now North Carolina), failed as a result of their troubles with the Indians and of their poor management during the years 1585–1591. It was here that the first English child was born in the colonies. This first "new American" was Virginia Dare.

No women were aboard the ships that carried 150 men to found

Two artists' interpretations of the Indian princess Pocahontas. Above left, in a painting of her wedding to Jamestown colonist John Rolfe; right, in a statue by William Ordway Partridge. A painting depicting Indian life in the West (below) shows women at several different kinds of work.

Above, the arrival of the "tobacco brides," Englishwomen brought to Virginia, where they were auctioned off for 120 pounds of tobacco each.

Below, in addition to keeping house, caring for the children, making the clothing, farming, and seeing to other household chores, the colonial woman had to make her own candles by a long, tedious process.

the first permanent settlement, called Jamestown, in Virginia in 1607. The Indians who met the settlers were hostile, but one of them, an Indian princess named Pocahontas, became their guardian angel. Pocahontas saved the life of Captain John Smith, became a Christian, and married one of the settlers, John Rolfe. Rolfe, who introduced tobacco planting into the New World, took his wife with him to England, where they were received by the royal family.

Women at Jamestown

Two women arrived at Jamestown colony during its second year. One was the wife of an original settler and the other, Anne Burrows, was her servant. Anne Burrows and a colonist probably took part in the first marriage ceremony performed between Europeans in the colonies. During the early years, Virginia was composed entirely of males, except for the wives of some officials and a few settlers.

A bit later, however, it was felt that the men who had decided to remain in the new colony should be provided with family life. And so, in 1620, a ship carrying ninety young women from England landed in Virginia. These women were actually put up for auction! The price was 120 pounds of tobacco per woman. It is said that "the men in Virginia did willinglie and lovinglie receive the newcomers." These women became known as "the tobacco brides."

Women's Life in Colonial Days

Long years of Indian warfare and battling against the stubborn wilderness served only to strengthen the spirit of the colonial woman. In addition to working as a wife, mother, and nurse, the colonial woman had to raise poultry and vegetables, to prepare butter and cheese, and to make soap and candles. A farmer without a wife was severely handicapped, for he had no one to make clothing or to help with the planting and harvesting or even to assist in fighting wild animals or Indians. Marriage, however, did not improve women's standing in the eyes of the law. Women did not have the right to own and inherit property, to make contracts, or to sue.

Women did become shopkeepers during the colonial days, and served also as schoolteachers and dressmakers. Others became innkeepers, ferry tenders, and wharf proprietors, and some women even became wholesale merchants and shipowners. In the South, Eliza Lucas Pinckney and Margaret Brent were managers of large plantations. Even at this early stage in our country's life, there were women who had decided to demand their rights to establish businesses and to compete on an equal standing with men.

An example of what the men thought of this activity appeared in the *North Carolina Gazette*, an early colonial newspaper, which printed this little poem:

> Make him *believe* he holds Sov'reign sway
> And she may *rule* by making him *obey*.

This old notion of "feminine wiles" was more easily accepted than open competition or equality.

Indian women and black women fared even worse than their white sisters in the early days of America's history. The Indian woman was considered as an inferior and an enemy, while the black woman was a slave.

THE PILGRIM WOMEN AT PLYMOUTH
(1620) AND PURITAN WOMEN AT
MASSACHUSETTS BAY (1625)

Why were these women willing to brave the storms of the Atlantic? Why were they willing to face what they knew would be a wild and hostile land, where nothing but suffering awaited them? They were searching for religious freedom from the persecution they had endured in their native land, England.

A PILGRIM WOMAN ASSERTS HERSELF

Captain Miles Standish wanted to marry Priscilla Mullins and thought, of course, that she would be flattered to marry a man of such high standing. But, too timid to ask for himself, he sent John Alden to propose for him. Priscilla, intent upon marrying John Alden, replied to his proposal from Standish, "Prithee, John, why do you not speak for yourself?" Result: Priscilla Mullins and John Alden became husband and wife.

For the black woman, slavery was the usual course. And with slavery could come brutal physical treatment. Above, a female slave is branded, like cattle. Below, Pilgrims at Provincetown observe their first Monday washday, November 23, 1620.

ELIZA LUCAS PINCKNEY (1723–1793)
WOMAN PLANTER

Eliza Lucas Pinckney made a major contribution to the economic life of the Carolinas. As a seventeen-year-old, she took over complete management of her father's plantations. Eliza experimented with crops other than rice. She developed indigo—a seed used for making a blue dye. This crop became the second most important export of the Carolinas. She also found time to study the classics, to instruct her sisters and black children in reading, to practice the piano, and to do needlework. Despite their accomplishments, however, such southern women helped maintain the system of slavery.

ANNE HUTCHINSON (c. 1591–1643)—
WOMAN DISSENTER
IN COLONIAL AMERICA

Anne Hutchinson, a woman of ready wit and bold spirit, rebelled against the harsh rules of New England Puritanism. In her speeches and in her writings she struck the first blow for religious freedom in America. The Massachusetts records state "she was too brilliant, too ambitious and too progressive for the ministers and magistrates of the colony . . . who feared her leadership." The women who attended Anne Hutchinson's lectures began to question the tyrannical rule of the males of the colony. Husbands began to notice that their wives became "strangely disputatious." As a result, Anne Hutchinson was expelled from the Massachusetts colony.

Although Anne Hutchinson was expelled from the Massachusetts Bay colony for her outspoken views on religious freedom and on the treatment of women, this statue was eventually erected in her honor.

2

WOMEN AND THE AMERICAN REVOLUTION

Women Before the
American Revolution

Between 1760 and 1775, an advertisement in the newspapers of Charleston, South Carolina, and Williamsburg, Virginia, read, "Dry Goods and Millinery Sale." The advertisers were women, thirty-six in Charleston and thirteen in Williamsburg. These first women merchants were the forerunners of the women in American fashion.

From Massachusetts to Virginia during the period before the Revolution, there were five women newspaper editors. When John Peter Zenger was jailed by the British in an effort to suppress his "rebellious" editorials, his wife, Anna Zenger, published and edited the New York *Weekly Journal*.

America's first poet was a woman, Ann Bradstreet, a farm wife with eight children, whose verses were published in London in 1650.

On the other hand, women made no headway as either lawyers or doctors. They did administer medication to their own families and worked as midwives and as practical nurses. And while no colony permitted them to vote, neither did women organize to seek this right.

They did, however, support the rebellion against the repressive laws made by England. Some colonial women banded together with the men in their efforts to force the English Parliament to repeal objectionable laws through economic pressure. The Daughters of Liberty and other women's societies advocated the making and wearing of colonial-made (homespun) clothes and discouraged the wearing of foreign-made dresses. They boycotted the use of English-taxed tea and imports. American women sat at their spinning wheels and pledged themselves to buy only domestic products.

In Philadelphia a women's relief organization headed by Esther

This drawing of "A Society of Patriotic Ladies, at Edenton in North Carolina," shows that women were not taken seriously in important matters. In the center of the picture a man makes advances toward a signer of the declaration to boycott English goods.

Reed and Sarah Franklin Bache, the daughter of Benjamin Franklin, collected funds to buy supplies for soldiers. More than sixteen hundred women were engaged in this project.

Martha Washington, Abigail Adams, and Mercy Otis Warren were the first women to be powerful influences in American history. The three women were totally different from one another in their personalities, activities, and abilities, but all were valuable advisers and counselors to their husbands.

Martha Washington, who as Martha Custis had inherited vast estates from her first husband, reflected the luxury and opulence of the South. As the wife of George Washington, she turned to the management of her estates in Virginia while at the same time joining him to brave the harsh winter at Valley Forge. It has been said that she heard the first cannon shot at Boston and the last at Yorktown.

By contrast, Abigail Adams represented the austerity of New England. She was selected along with Mercy Otis Warren and Hannah Winthrop to try to discover which of their friends and neighbors were pro-British. Many leaders consulted with Abigail Adams before meeting with her husband, John Adams. Abigail Adams sent reports of the preparations for the battles near Boston. John Adams wrote to his wife, "You are really brave, my dear. You are a heroine." Their son John Quincy Adams said of his mother, "my mother with her infant children dwelt, liable every hour of the day and night to be butchered in cold blood or taken into Boston as a hostage." But Abigail chided her husband when he was at the Continental Congress in Philadelphia in 1776 discussing the "rights of *mankind*." She wrote, "you insist upon retaining an absolute power over wives." Later, John Adams admitted that women should not be relegated to purely personal and domestic concerns.

Mercy Otis Warren was a vigorous propagandist, playwright, and

During the American Revolution, Esther Reed (above) organized Philadelphia women to collect money with which to buy goods for soldiers in the colonial army. Martha Custis Washington, in a painting by Gilbert Stuart (center), was one of the wealthiest women in Virginia when she married George Washington. American author Mercy Otis Warren (below) wrote extensively for the colonists' cause in the Revolution. Among her associates were Thomas Jefferson and Samuel, John, and Abigail Adams. She was recognized for her writing and intellectual abilities.

satirist of the American Revolution, as well as its first woman historian.

She wielded a deep influence upon the thinking of her time, stating her belief that, ". . . American daughters are politicians and patriots." But during the American Revolution and the early years under the Constitution, women did not take organized action to correct the inequalities in their rights. Even the famous and liberal Philadelphian Dr. Benjamin Rush had said to a young friend about to be married, ". . . from the day you marry, you must have no will of your own."

Not all black people were in bondage during Revolutionary times. Phillis Wheatley was a young slave who had been born in Africa and was purchased by a Boston tailor whose family treated her well and provided her with an education. Before the Revolution, Phillis took a trip to England, where some of her poems were published. Returning to Boston free, she married another freed slave in 1778, and wrote her most famous poem, "Liberty and Peace." These are the final lines of the poem:

> Auspicious Heaven shall fill with fav'ring Gales
> Wher e'er Columbia spreads her swelling sails,
> To every Realm shall peace her charms display
> And Heavenly Freedom spread her Golden Day.

Women in the
American Revolution

When the men marched off to fight in the Revolution, their wives and daughters took up their duties in the fields and on the farms. They maintained the ships and factories, supplying the armies with the necessities of life and war. In the South, many women took over the responsibilities of the plantations, directing the slaves and running businesses. As stated earlier, women are not blameless in that ugly page of American history. The entire life pattern of women began to change as they demonstrated their ability to assume what had been considered masculine duties and responsibilities.

The real story of Molly Pitcher's loading of her husband's cannon when he was unable to fight on is now lost in folklore, but she was actually on the scene and served bravely. Rebecca Biddle, the wife of Colonel Clement Biddle, joined the army along with her husband. Lucy Knox, the wife of Major Henry Knox, followed the army and was a strong and steady support to her husband. Women showed their

African-born Phillis Wheatley began her life in America as a slave but became an accomplished poet who read her work before royalty in England.

courage and influence before the actual fighting began as well as in the years that followed.

Two women, Sally St. Clair of South Carolina and Deborah Sampson of Massachusetts, dressed in men's clothing and served as soldiers. Margaret Corbin received a soldier's pension from Congress for stepping into the role of artillery soldier when her husband was killed.

A WOMAN SPY IN THE
AMERICAN REVOLUTION

Early in the war, General George Washington learned that women spies could be as ardent and efficient as men, and much less readily suspected. When the American army was at Valley Forge in 1777, the British, under General William Howe, were enjoying Philadelphia's hospitality at the home of a family called Darragh. Their daughter Lydia overheard British officers planning an attack on Washington's army. Using the excuse of buying flour to get through the British troops, Lydia passed some papers hidden in needlework to an American colonel. The papers revealed that the British were planning to attack from Philadelphia. General Washington, using this information from Lydia Darragh, launched his own attack and defeated the British.

Disguised as a man, Deborah Sampson (left) served in the Revolution under the name Robert Shurtleff with the Massachusetts regiment. She later published The Female Review, *the story of her army experience. A painting of Margaret Cochran Corbin (right), who heroically served in the American Revolution. When her husband died in action, during the Battle of Fort Washington, she took his place with the First Company of Pennsylvania Artillery until she too was badly wounded.*

3

WOMEN
GO WEST

By wagon train, riverboat, stagecoach, on horseback, and on foot, many women went west. Some went to work, some went to marry, and some went seeking adventure. Women accompanied their husbands in covered wagons. Many lost their lives, some were even captured by Indians. Some were never heard from again.

When they had established their new homes, few women attained fame outside of their own communities. Most of them attended strictly to what was considered "the business of women." This meant keeping up their husbands' courage, rearing children, performing the household duties of cooking, washing and ironing, and sewing, all without modern conveniences, of course. They made candles, soap, and yeast, feeding the hired hands and working in the fields when necessary.

Most pioneer women went west because their husbands did. Life was almost unbearable in their sod huts or log cabins, where they were buffeted by cold winds and harsh weather. They had the courage to bear all of their burdens, for they wanted to build stable communities out of the wild and untamed wilderness. They worked tirelessly until their land, their homes, and their families were safe.

Among the unknown and brave women who went west were missionaries and nuns who worked among both Indian and white fam-

Above, a wagon train resting along a riverbank on the Oregon Trail. Women and children traveled this way despite severe hardships. Below, the Shores family of Custer County, Nebraska, in front of their sod house, which was dark and dusty. In time the family plastered and whitewashed their home.

ilies. There were even young women from New England who had heard that some of the areas in the West had an abundance of marriageable young men.

SACAGAWEA, INDIAN GUIDE

Sacagawea, a young Indian woman, was the interpreter and guide for the Lewis and Clark Expedition to the Pacific Ocean between 1804 and 1806. She was born among the Shoshoni (Snake) Indians. Enemy Indians had captured her and sold her as a slave to a French-Canadian trader—Toussaint Charbonneau. Despite having a newborn child, Sacagawea went along with Lewis and Clark. While the expedition was crossing the continental divide, the explorers met relatives of Sacagawea among the Shoshoni. She was able to supply the expedition with food and horses. Sacagawea actually made it possible for the expedition to continue its journey to the Pacific Ocean and back. Her role as ambassador of peace and friend was stated by Clark, "She reconciles all the Indians to our friendly tribes. A woman with a party of men is a token of peace."

When disaster struck, everyone pitched in. Above, women and children help to clear a field of grasshoppers that ate the settlers' crops.

Below, a painting of the Lewis and Clark Expedition. On the right is the artist's rendition of Sacagawea, the young Indian guide and interpreter who accompanied the explorers.

4

WOMEN IN THE FIGHT AGAINST SLAVERY

Black women in America suffered under slavery as badly as men. Women slaves, separated from their husbands and children, worked long hours in the fields and the homes of their owners.

The antislavery movement caught the attention and won the support of many American women in the years between the American Revolution and outbreak of the Civil War. These women were determined to establish equal rights for all people in the United States, as had been guaranteed by the Constitution. To them, this meant first and foremost, the abolition of slavery. The modern women's rights movement can truly be said to be an offshoot of the antislavery organizations. For the first time, women had organized to combat existing practices and laws that condoned inequality by reason of color. Later, it was to be by reason of their just being women.

The American Anti-Slavery Society had many white women supporters. Among those who fought bravely for abolition were the Quaker minister Lucretia Mott and her friends Sarah and Angelina Grimké. The Grimké sisters, who had had a conventional southern upbringing, knew at firsthand the horrors of slavery. They became Quakers and moved to Philadelphia where they joined Lucretia Mott in the abolitionist movement.

Black slave women were given three major types of work. Some worked in the fields (above left); others worked ginning cotton (above right); and still others worked as house slaves (below left). All, however, were slaves. Below right: Angelina (left) and Sarah Grimké left the South, where they were daughters of rich South Carolina slaveholders, to work against slavery. They spoke out and wrote against the institution of slavery and for equality for women. Sarah Grimké championed the workingwoman and demanded "Equal pay for equal work!"

Above, Harriet Tubman, "the Moses of her people," as a young woman and in old age. Sojourner Truth (below) was a speaker whom audiences never forgot when she argued against slavery.

Black women and former slaves lectured, wrote, and helped others escape from slavery on the "Underground Railroad." Sojourner Truth and Harriet Tubman, ex-slaves, were heroic in the battle against slavery.

In 1837, there were 1,006 abolition groups with more than one hundred thousand members, of which women made up more than half. Many women received their political and "soapbox" training from the antislavery movement.

It was, perhaps, Harriet Beecher Stowe's novel *Uncle Tom's Cabin* that struck the greatest single antislavery blow in this country.

FIGHTERS FOR FREEDOM

Harriet Tubman (c. 1820–1913)—"the Moses of her people"— was an escaped slave. She was the most celebrated "conductor" on the Underground Railroad. She made nineteen trips to the South in ten years and led more than three hundred slaves to freedom. A price of $40,000 was placed on her head. Her capture in the South would probably have meant instant death. She was never caught. During the Civil War she served as a scout for the Union Army.

Sojourner Truth (1797–1893) was born a slave named Isabella Baumfree. She was sold together with a herd of sheep. When New York State abolished slavery for adults in 1817, she was freed. She became a preacher and took the name "Sojourner Truth." After the Civil War, she was appointed by the Freedmen's Bureau to train black women for employment.

When she was eighty years old she boarded Jim Crow (segregated) streetcars in Washington, D.C., and seated herself in the white section. She was forcibly thrown off by the conductors. She saw to it that each such incident became a lesson in cruelty and inhumanity that white observers would not forget.

Jane Swisshelm (1815–1884) was an outspoken journalist and editor of the *St. Cloud Visitor* and *The Democrat* in Minnesota. Because she accused a political leader of proslavery sentiments, her office and press were destroyed and the type was thrown into the river. But she continued her campaign against slavery and for the rights of women.

5

WOMEN IN THE CIVIL WAR

As with every major conflict in America's history, the Civil War saw great advances in women's status and opportunities. President Lincoln recognized women by giving them certain minor jobs in government departments. But it was not until 1870 that women were officially welcomed into federal service.

At the outbreak of the Civil War, women in the North began to organize ladies aid societies. They made bandages, underwear, towels, blankets, and other supplies. In New York City fifty or sixty of these groups under the leadership of Dr. Elizabeth Blackwell formed the Women's Central Association for Relief. In the South there were also numerous state and county relief associations.

Susan B. Anthony, who fought for temperance (no alcohol) and votes for women, and Elizabeth Stanton, who later became a leader in the women's rights movement, took the lead in organizing the Women's Loyal National League to support the war effort and to pressure for the freeing of the slaves. When President Lincoln met Harriet Beecher Stowe, the author of *Uncle Tom's Cabin*, he is supposed to have said, "So this is the little lady who caused the great war." Two outstanding women during this time were Julia Ward Howe, who wrote the "Battle Hymn of the Republic" and Clara Barton, who organized a volunteer nurse corps for wounded and disabled soldiers and later founded the American Red Cross.

Dr. Elizabeth Blackwell (above left), the first woman to graduate from a medical school in the United States, organized groups of women in New York to make supplies for Union soldiers during the Civil War. Harriet Beecher Stowe (above right) never lived in the South, but she heard stories from former slaves and as a result wrote Uncle Tom's Cabin, *a powerful weapon against slavery. Clara Barton, founder of the American Red Cross, shown below at the time of the Civil War, during which she organized a volunteer nurse corps.*

In their efforts to help during the Civil War, women often masqueraded as men and enlisted in the Blues (Union) and Grays (Confederate). Although this playacting was usually detected, a Canadian girl, Sarah Emma Edmonds, survived the war as a soldier with a Michigan regiment. Nurses, wives, and sisters of soldiers tried to pass information to both sides, but most of it was gossip and therefore useless.

It may be said that as with freed slaves, southern women were "liberated" by the Civil War. They picked up the pieces of their shattered lives and helped to reconstruct southern society. After the Civil War, both black and white women worked as teachers in freedmen's schools, as pension claim agents, and as rehabilitation workers with soldiers and refugees.

SPIES IN THE CIVIL WAR

Belle Boyd, an eighteen-year-old southerner, delivered information to General Stonewall Jackson revealing a Union Army plan to attack Fort Royal in the Shenandoah Valley of Virginia. This revelation enabled the Confederate General Jackson to mount a successful attack against the Union Army. In a letter to Belle Boyd, General Jackson expressed his gratitude and admiration of her bravery. She was later captured and imprisoned by the Union army, but not executed, since it was the policy of the military at that time not to put female spies to death.

Pauline Cushman was an actress who served as a Union spy. She praised Jefferson Davis, the President of the Confederacy, from the stage in Louisville, Kentucky, at the same time she was passing information to the North. She was finally caught and sentenced to be executed as a Union spy. However, the arrival of Union troops saved her life.

Sarah Emma Edmonds (left) served as a soldier during the Civil War. Actress Pauline Cushman (right) served as a Union spy in the Civil War.

Sarah Thompson, a widow from Tennessee and the mother of two small girls, was a strong Unionist. Working against the Confederacy, she gathered information to pass on to the Union army. In one instance she alerted the Union army as to where they could find General John Hunt Morgan, a Confederate leader of guerrilla troops. The Union army surprised and defeated the guerrillas at Greenville, Tennessee. General Morgan was ambushed and shot as he hurried out in his nightclothes to round up his troops. When she died, Ms. Thompson was buried at Arlington National Cemetery with full military honors.

Rose O'Neal Greenhow, a widow living in Washington, was sympathetic toward the South. Early in the conflict, Ms. Greenhow managed to send couriers through the Union lines with a message that the Union army was marching on Manassas, Virginia. Thus forewarned, the Confederate army was able to set the stage for the first Union defeat at the first Battle of Bull Run in 1861. Ms. Greenhow was arrested by the pioneer detective Allan E. Pinkerton. Because of the illness of her eight-year-old daughter, who was with her in jail, Ms. Greenhow was freed from prison and sent to Richmond.

Elizabeth Van Lew rescued Union prisoners from the prison in Richmond, Virginia. She posed as an eccentric and was known as "Crazy Bet." Meanwhile she gathered military information and forwarded it to General Ulysses S. Grant. At the end of the Civil War she was appointed postmistress of Richmond as a reward for her services as a spy.

6

WOMEN FIGHT FOR THEIR RIGHTS

The Absence of Rights for Women

It was still a man's world at the beginning of the 1800's. Like black slaves, women couldn't vote, and they could be legally beaten by their "overlords," their husbands. They could not keep ownership of their property when they married.

Since the position of women was inferior to that of men, their rights were equally inferior. Very few girls received an education. The only occupations open to them were teaching, factory work, and domestic work—all very poorly paid.

The average young woman was "married off" by her father at an early age. She then spent the rest of her life keeping house and rearing a family. Compared with today, this was "hard labor." For at that time, of course, almost everything had to be made or done by hand. The broom and the washboard were the two available household aids. The woman of the early 1800's possessed few legal rights. All valuables or property she had and any wages she earned went to her husband. Her children were also her husband's legal responsibility. He was given custody of the children in the event of divorce, and he could name their guardian at his death. If the husband left property, his widow often had to appoint a man to take care of it for her.

Certainly, these political, social, educational, economic, and legal inequalities cried out for reform.

The Women's Rights Movement "Takes Off"

By 1850 the movement for women's rights was fortified by a bold Scotswoman, Frances "Fanny" Wright. She dared to speak on the subjects of antislavery, better education for women, and control by women of their own property all over the United States. A few cour-

ageous women followed her example. They called themselves *feminists*, from the Latin word *femina* meaning "woman."

These first feminists demanded the right to vote and insisted upon educational and job reforms. Among them, some urged temperance and antislavery reform. The reformers had received encouragement from the example of such European women as the English suffragist Mary Wollstonecraft.

The women's rights movement in the last half of the nineteenth century was led by some unusual women. Prominent among them were:

LUCRETIA MOTT (1793–1880)

a Quaker, who first publicly
advocated equal rights for women.

ELIZABETH CADY STANTON (1815–1902)

a mother of seven who had insisted
upon leaving the word "obey" out
of her marriage ceremony,
and who advocated votes for women.

SUSAN B. ANTHONY (1820–1906)

a militant lecturer for women's rights,
who demanded the right to vote.

LUCY STONE (1818–1893)

who kept her maiden name in marriage
and lectured on women's rights
and the abolition of slavery.

Husbands and fathers often had total control over a woman's life in the 1800's. The drawing above shows a father introducing his daughter to Papa's choice of her future husband. Lucretia Mott (below) who lectured in favor of women's suffrage and in opposition to slavery and alcohol, often met angry and violent mobs.

AMELIA BLOOMER (1818–1894)
who revolted against the "street
sweeping female dress," wore
man-like short skirts with Turkish
trousers, or "bloomers," and
fought for the right to vote.

The Struggle for the Right to Vote
In 1848, at Seneca Falls, New York, about three hundred feminists
held a Women's Rights Convention. In a revision of the Declaration
of Independence stating that "All men and *women* are created equal,"
they listed many grievances (complaints) against men. Their pri-
mary demand was that America grant its women the right to vote.
The "suffragettes," as they were called, gave notice to the country
that they were ready and willing to fight for that right.

After the Civil War (1861–1865) the freed American black male
was given the right to vote by the Constitution. Now, America's female reformers turned to women's rights. Above all was the cry for
their right to vote.

When Susan Anthony voted illegally in the presidential election of
1872, she was arrested and taken to court. At her trial, she was found
guilty and fined.

*Elizabeth Cady Stanton (above left), who lived in Seneca Falls, New
York, organized the 1848 women's rights convention held there. She
was regarded as the "mother" of the women's suffrage movement.
Center left, Susan B. Anthony's Quaker family introduced her to the
idea of women's rights and won her over to the cause. She and Elizabeth Cady Stanton were leaders of the women's movement of their
time. Ms. Anthony was a teacher, writer, and newspaper editor. She
headed the National American Woman Suffrage Association between
1892 and 1900. Below left, suffragist Lucy Stone was an effective
writer and speaker for women's rights. Right, Amelia Bloomer fought
for women's suffrage and against women's traditional and cumber-
some clothing. She is shown here in the fashion that bears her name.*

The content of a proposed suffrage amendment to the Constitution was written by Susan Anthony and introduced in Congress in 1878. Forty-two years later, in its original form, it became the Nineteenth Amendment to the Constitution.

The victory for women's suffrage was gradual. Before 1900, four western states—Wyoming, Colorado, Utah, and Idaho—granted women the right to vote on the state level. During the first part of the twentieth century, under the leadership of Carrie Chapman Catt, seven more states gave women the vote. In 1917, Montana elected Jeanette Rankin as the first woman to the United States House of Representatives. Throughout the country there were parades, picketing, and words—printed and spoken—to demand the right to vote. "Votes for women" was the slogan. And even the bad eggs and bad words that were hurled did not stop them.

Another war—World War I—in which women were actively involved as nurses, doctors, factory workers, army aides, and Red Cross workers brought forth the Nineteenth Amendment. Passed in 1920, it established the right of women to vote in national as well as in state elections. In 1971, all eighteen-year-olds, regardless of their sex, were granted the same voting rights.

Women Make Progress in Education

The colonial elementary schools offered boys and girls the same basic subjects. However, throughout the first half of the 1800's, secondary schools for girls were private and were known as "seminaries." As far back as those days, one school for girls, the Female Seminary of Troy, New York, made what was considered a "strange" statement. This school, established in 1821, argued that mental exertion would *not* damage a woman's brain. The school's directors pro-

Above, leaders at the executive committee meeting to plan an international suffrage meeting in 1888. In the front row, Susan B. Anthony is seated second from the left; Elizabeth Cady Stanton is third from the right. Below, when the territory of Wyoming was admitted to the Union in 1890, women there had already been voting and taking an active part in local politics for twenty years.

posed a similar education for both boys and girls, an idea that shocked early educators.

In the 1830's, Prudence Crandall, a Quaker from Connecticut, operated a school that admitted black girls. Despite threats and difficulties, she persisted. Mary Lyon, a prominent woman educator, founded Mount Holyoke Seminary in 1837. Today, Mount Holyoke College admits boys into its classes.

The first public high school for girls opened in Worcester, Massachusetts, in 1824. The number of such schools increased in the succeeding years. Soon, coeducation was accepted as the proper form of public education.

Violent disagreements raged during the nineteenth century over higher education for women. Should women go to college? Should they go to women's colleges? Should they take the same subjects as men?

In 1837, Oberlin College accepted its first women applicants, both white and black. Other private colleges for women opened after the Civil War. Among them were Vassar, Smith, Wellesley, and Bryn Mawr. Pressures from prominent women in both public and professional life finally forced America's universities into opening their doors to women by the end of the 1800's. Women were admitted not only to general studies, but also to the professional courses, leading to the granting of degrees in medicine, architecture, and the applied sciences. Over the years, however, the number of women admitted into professional schools has remained relatively small.

The increased opportunities for women helped to bring about a social revolution. In 1849, Elizabeth Blackwell became the first American woman to receive a doctor of medicine degree. She had applied to twenty-nine medical schools before finally being accepted. Women are now admitted into every profession and are hired by all but the building and shiploading (stevedoring) trades.

Today in the United States, while most schools are coeducational,

Mary Lyon (above), founder of Mount Holyoke College in Massachusetts, made certain that the school's standards were as high as possible. The dining hall at Oberlin College (below), after the Ohio school pioneered in admitting women to an institution of higher learning.

the curriculum for boys and girls frequently differs. Separate courses are still conducted for boys in mechanical and technical subjects. Stenography courses are usually attended only by girls. Some of these differences are because of attitudes or customs, which are very difficult to change.

AMERICAN WOMEN IN EDUCATION

· A greater proportion of girls than boys complete secondary education.

BUT only about:
· 38 percent of the undergraduate students at college are female.

· 62 percent of the undergraduate students at college are male.
· Fewer females than males become candidates for master's degrees.
· 11.6 percent of earned doctorates (Ph.D.) are held by women.
· American women are not participating in higher education to the degree that they should.

Women's Organizations and Clubs for Reform
The nineteenth-century woman worked hard and long in a great variety of movements, from eliminating poverty to improving the world's environment. Women's organizations became deeply involved in bringing aid to orphans, the deaf, the mentally ill, the blind, the poor, and the sick. Dorothea Dix was one of the early advocates in America for social reform.

Among the many objectives sought by women's organizations was the protection of families against the abuses of drunken men. The seriousness of alcoholism was portrayed in articles and plays describing the destruction of whole families as a result of drunkenness. As a consequence, direct and strong action was taken against the liquor industry. Women were shown praying outside of bars and taverns for their husbands' reform. In 1874, Frances Willard organized the Women's Christian Temperance Union, which campaigned for alcohol education and awakened the public to the evils of alcoholic abuse. Suffragist Carrie Chapman Catt was influential in the movement, which led to the passage of the Eighteenth Amendment (the Prohibition Amendment) in 1917. It was repealed in 1933.

Women had been easily aroused to fight against the abuses of drinking liquor. They were just as easily won over to the cause of "emancipation of women," most especially with respect to giving them the right to vote. They pursued this cause to the passage of the Nineteenth Amendment.

Religion was another field in which women were active, raising funds to convert people to Christianity. They served as missionaries to many foreign countries. The Young Women's Christian Association (YWCA) was organized to provide classes, recreation, and housing for women.

A distinctive "women's development" has been the "women's club." Some clubs emphasize literary and cultural activities. Others concern themselves with such social improvements as the elimination of poverty, the establishment of day-care centers for children, and slum clearance. With the passage of the Nineteenth Amendment in 1920, many women's organizations have become involved in politics. The chief concern of many women's clubs is to ensure women equal rights, especially in the field of employment. Others emphasize civil rights—equal treatment regardless of race or national origin. The peace movement also has emerged as an objective that women's clubs endorse.

The League of Women Voters seeks to instruct women in the workings of government. While the league does participate in promoting the passage of legislation, it does not engage in partisan politics. The National Organization for Women (NOW) was founded in 1963. It is a major women's rights group organized on a national basis. NOW seeks to work for "true equality for all women in America and toward a fully equal partnership of the sexes as part of the worldwide revolution of human rights now taking place within and beyond our national borders."

JANE ADDAMS (1860–1935)

Settlement houses were established to provide solutions to some of the problems of the immigrants who came to the cities toward the end of the 1800's. Famous among them was Chicago's Hull House, founded in 1889 by Jane Addams. Her goal was to feed the hungry, to care for the sick, and to provide recreation for the old and education for the young. At Hull House, immigrants were helped in finding and establishing homes and in learning English. Today Hull House stands as a beacon in the world of social work. It continues to provide services beyond those given by the government in social security, housing, welfare, and medicare.

Emma Willard (above left), who pioneered in women's education, founded the Troy Female Seminary, where young women were taught the same subjects as were young men. Social worker Jane Addams (above right), founder of Chicago's Hull House, the first social settlement of its kind in the United States. The YWCA led the way in providing many types of instruction for women: communications (center), photography (below left), and typewriting (below right).

7

WOMEN IN THE LABOR MOVEMENT

Women workers have always had to combat male prejudice. We have seen that even in colonial days, while women were chiefly home-makers, there were women throughout the colonies who did every-thing from managing farms and estates to publishing newspapers. But today there is still an ongoing battle for equality in employment and compensation, goals that are foremost in the minds of all women workers.

Most nineteenth-century women considered marriage to be their most important "job." Seldom employed outside the home, the average nineteenth-century woman worked very hard at rearing her children and running her household smoothly. She was not for the most part a wage earner. Then, when the cotton mills came to New England in the 1820's and 1830's, the picture changed, especially for young daughters of local farmers. For the first time they could gain employment in the mills, outside of the home, and look forward to something other than marriage and a family. By 1828, women made up 41.1 percent of the employees in the seven largest woolen mills, and by 1838 this figure had risen to 49 percent. In the cotton mills, the percentage of women employees was considerably larger.

By 1840, women had organized unions among textile workers, tailors, seamstresses, umbrella sewers, bookbinders, and clothing and

Above, during the 1860 shoemakers' strike in Lynn, Massachusetts, women joined the protest. Their sign reads, "American ladies will not be slaves. Give us a fair compensation and we labour cheerfully."

New England factories gave women the opportunity to work outside their homes, but the work was hard, the hours long, and conditions poor. In the picture below, children and women of all ages can be seen in front of the factory.

shoe workers. Later, in order to improve working conditions and wage scales for women, other unions were organized in the cigar, printing, and laundry industries. However, women employees earned far less than men for equal work in the same industries.

From the Civil War to World War I (1865 to 1914), the number of employed women in American business increased, while the number of those working on farms decreased. To quote figures, in 1890, 3.7 million women were holding jobs. By 1910, this number had increased to more than 8 million. By 1914, 21.1 percent of all those employed in the United States were women.

FRANCES PERKINS (1882–1965)

Frances Perkins, the first woman member of the U.S. Cabinet in history, was appointed Secretary of Labor in 1933 by President Franklin Delano Roosevelt. She served in this post for twelve years, a longer period than any other person. A graduate of Mount Holyoke College, she had a long record in the field of labor. The most famous case in which she was involved was the 1911 Triangle factory fire in New York, in which 145 workers, mostly women, lost their lives. Frances Perkins directed the investigation of the fire for the New York State Factory Commission in 1912–1913, which found that a lack of safety conditions had caused the great loss of life. Ms. Perkins had taught school, worked at Hull House, and been New York State Industrial Commissioner. Although married, she always used her maiden name.

Women and men, mostly immigrants, worked under terrible conditions in "sweatshops" (above and center) around the turn of the century. Frances B. Perkins, who served as secretary of labor for twelve years, shown below with the late President John F. Kennedy.

8

WOMEN IN THE TWO WORLD WARS

War and its effect on the family have always been of deep concern to women. Even though each war in American history has led to further emancipation (freedom), each has also brought sorrow.

The American Revolution started American women on the road to freedom. They learned to ask questions about the government for which they performed brave and patriotic deeds. The Civil War drew women into jobs. Some went to the battlefields and hospitals. The Spanish-American War saw the beginning of a formal nursing corps and the spread of Red Cross activities on the battlefields.

World War I

During the United States participation in World War I (1917–1918), women were once again actively involved. They were nurses, Red Cross workers, money-raisers, and factory workers. It was during World War I that women learned that they could hold down jobs and function ably in occupations that were previously reserved exclusively for men.

The Nineteenth Amendment gave women the right to vote in national and state elections. It was approved by Congress and the states in 1920, partly because of women's service during World War I but chiefly because of their militancy. Women picketed and were assaulted and jailed in their fight for the right to vote.

Above left, Red Cross nurses on the way to battlefields in Cuba during the Spanish-American War in 1898. Above right, a Red Cross nurse working during World War I. Demanding the right to vote (center) and exercising it for the first time (below).

New Women of the Twenties

The "new woman" of the 1920's wanted the same freedom as a man. She sought the right to determine her own style of life, to improve society, and to choose a profession. She felt that this could be accomplished along with, or instead of, marriage and children. The 1920's woman felt free to smoke, dance, wear makeup, and to drink and act in ways that her mother had not dreamed of.

Among the women of the twenties were such heroes as Gertrude Ederle, who swam the English Channel, and Amelia Earhart, the first woman to fly the Atlantic. Not every girl, however, was a "flapper," or new woman, with bared knees and painted lips.

World War II

While the United States was involved in World War II (1941–1945), women again answered the nation's call. As they had responded during World War I, once again they filled jobs in industry, government, and in the noncombatant armed services. At the outset of World War II, women were told that it was their patriotic duty to fill the jobs vacated by soldiers. They worked in munition factories and at jobs never before performed by women. "Rosie the Riveter" became a national symbol, as women became welders, machinists, and truck drivers or took other jobs that had always been considered "men's work."

Many occupations were filled by women who were replacing men called into service during and after World War II. Included were such jobs as those of accountants, engineers, and lawyers. But their numbers have remained small because of discrimination. In the business world women still tended to be confined to such tasks as stenography, secretarial work, telephone operating, retail selling, restaurant services, attendants in doctors' and dentists' offices, nursing, textile work, canning and assembly-line work.

Above, Amelia Earhart, the first woman to fly across the Atlantic.

Women in uniform and out did their share of the work during World War II (below and on page 52).

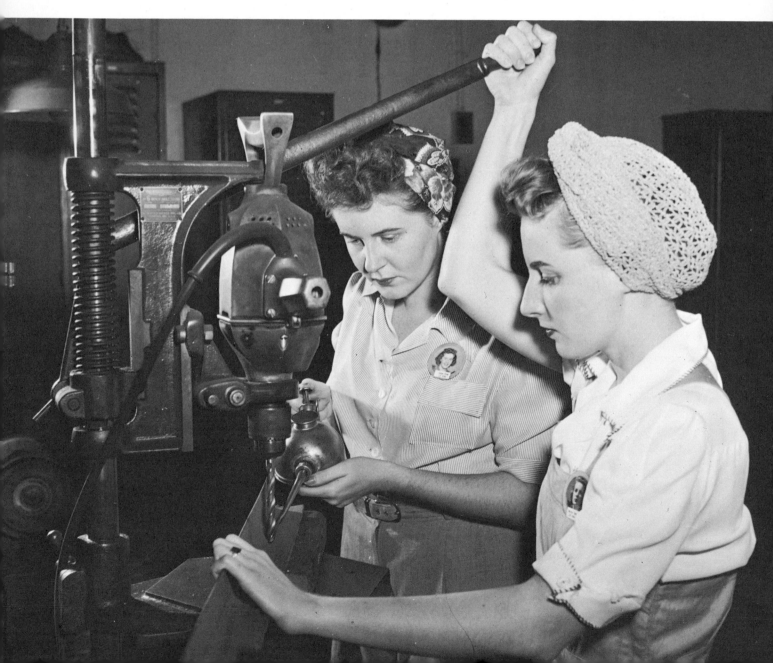

A million women replaced men in industry during World War II. Black women workers were paid $10 a week less than whites in the same jobs. And, after the war black women employees were the first to be let go.

```
WOMEN'S EARNINGS
MEDIAN INCOMES 1968
White women—$4,580
Black women—$3,487
White men—$7,870
Black men—$5,314
```

Women at the End of World War II

Other significant gains had been made in women's rights by the end of World War II. One of these was the right of women who had married foreigners to retain their citizenship (1924). The number of females who availed themselves of educational opportunities increased steadily. They remained in school longer.

Community property laws established equal property rights for married women. These laws automatically divided the family income and assets evenly between husband and wife. As a whole, in the United States, women are said to outrank men as property holders. The statistics, of course, include widows and children who have inherited estates from their deceased husbands and fathers. They show that 70 percent of the nation's property is held by women. Included in the holdings are stocks, insurance policies, and 65 percent of all savings accounts. These figures, however, do not reveal how much of these monies is actually controlled by men.

Latest census figures reveal that marriages are taking place at a later age—twenty-five years—and divorces are on the increase. Most divorces are granted to women, the majority of whom tend to marry again. The family still remains the symbol of security for both women and men.

A significant crusade for the world of the future was started by Margaret Sanger. Hers was a long fight for the right of women to obtain information about birth control. Margaret Sanger stated that it was the right of women to decide how many children they should bear. Together with medical advancements and improved means of contraception, it is hoped that control over the size of their families will enable women to make greater contributions to society as a whole. And it might be the answer to the world's population explosion.

Since World War I women have had not only the right to vote but have risen to serve as governors, members of Congress and of the Cabinet, and as ambassadors and in other high government positions. But there have been only a handful of women appointed to or elected to these positions. For most women job-holders, work lacks excitement, responsibility, challenge, and fair compensation. Now women have discovered that although their battle for the franchise was won, their war for complete equality was not. Discrimination in employment and education have continued.

ANNA ELEANOR ROOSEVELT (1884–1962)

One of the greatest of American women, Eleanor Roosevelt, played a more active role in national and international affairs than any other President's wife. During her years as America's First Lady, she greatly altered that role and was of tremendous importance to her husband, President Franklin Delano Roosevelt. Among other things she fought against discriminatory practices against minority groups.

Eleanor Roosevelt, a delegate to the first session of the United Nations, worked diligently to achieve United Nations' approval of the Declaration of Human Rights. She was the founder of Wiltwick School for deprived children.

Margaret Sanger began the crusade to gain women's rights to birth-control information. Above, in 1931, she pleads her cause before a Senate meeting.

Eleanor Roosevelt, at work at the United Nations (below).

9

CREATIVE WOMEN

From colonial times on, American women moved steadily into the forefront in the fields of literature, poetry, music, the arts, sculpture, theater, ballet, and fashion. Talented and ambitious women have grasped the opportunity for widespread success and approval. Women have written and published from colonial days to the present. While women have found their greatest opportunities in literature—poetry, novels, and journalism—they have also made conspicuous progress in other arts and sciences.

Poets

Not all heroes are armed with guns or swords. Many use their imaginations and pens to accomplish their ends, and among these are American women of talent and genius who turned to the writing of poetry. They used words as their "ammunition," enriching the world's literature as well as raising the status of women in general.

Phillis Wheatley, who rose from slavery, had her poetry published in 1773, when she was nineteen. Emily Dickinson received recognition only after her death in 1886. Her poems were called "the most readable, the most understandable and the most inspiring."

Edna St. Vincent Millay was a great lyric poet, whose sonnets have been compared favorably with the romantic poets of the time of Shakespeare. In 1923, she was the first woman awarded the Pulitzer Prize for poetry. In 1960, poet Gwendolyn Brooks became the first black writer awarded the Pulitzer Prize.

Kansas-born poet Gwendolyn Brooks won the 1950 Pulitzer Prize for poetry, one of several awards she has received. A Street in Bronzeville, Anne Allen, *and* Bronzeville Boys and Girls *are a few of her works.*

Novelists

American women knew that speaking was a powerful weapon in combating the prejudices of men against their participation in life outside the home. They soon began to realize that writing was even more potent, for it gave permanence to their opinions. Recognition came slowly, but today women are accepted in the literary field as equal to men.

Fiction writing has always been a favorite with women. Of the novels published before 1820 about one third were written by women. Sarah Wentworth in 1781 was the author of the first novel written in America. Best remembered today are Louisa M. Alcott's book *Little Women* (1868), which made girlhood, its problems, its urges, and its pleasures real for millions, and Harriet Beecher Stowe's *Uncle Tom's Cabin*, which was published in book form in 1852. America was shocked by Ms. Stowe's account of the cruelty and sorrows of slavery.

Willa Cather was one of the great writers of short stories and novels and of the twentieth century. Her stories dealt chiefly with her younger days.

Edith Wharton, in 1920, became the first woman to win the Pulitzer prize for literature, with her novel *The Age of Innocence*.

Pearl Buck has written novels based on her experiences as a missionary in China. *The Good Earth* established her as a world literary figure. In 1938 she was honored as the first and only American woman to be awarded the Nobel prize for literature.

Margaret Mitchell, Mary McCarthy, Eudora Welty, Joyce Carol Oates and Ellen Glasgow are but a few other prominent writers.

Playwrights

Women writers of dramatic works have been called "heroes without swords" for those plays that combine entertainment and messages.

Lillian Hellman's plays contain themes of human conflict. She was in the forefront in the fight for human rights in the twentieth century. *Watch on the Rhine* and *The Little Foxes* are but two of her contributions to the theater.

Lorraine Hansberry, a black American, devoted her all too short life to painting and writing. She is best known for her play *A Raisin in the Sun*. She died in 1965 at the age of thirty-five.

Three outstanding novelists: Louisa May Alcott (above), Willa Cather (left), and Pearl Buck (right).

The Arts

The arts have always been an open field of accomplishment for women. The study of painting was available to women at early established art schools. Schools for design in New England, New York, and Philadelphia have long existed.

Mary Cassatt was an outstanding American artist of the early twentieth century. She belonged to the impressionist school. In 1966, the United States government issued a commemorative postage stamp in her honor. One of her paintings "Maternité," was sold for $35,000.

Although Gertrude Stein was a writer, her fame in the twentieth century rests on her genius for recognizing such great talents in the art world as Picasso and Matisse. She surrounded herself with masterworks of modern art in her famous Paris salon.

Georgia O'Keefe is one of the greatest of American painters in the middle of the twentieth century. Her modern art is characterized by her use of color and clean lines. Her most beautiful paintings are of flowers, skulls, and barren hills.

The eminent sculptor Malvina Hoffman is known in the twentieth century for her busts of famous people and her dancing figures. In the Field Museum in Chicago are 110 bronze figures, which she created portraying the races of man.

The Performing Arts

A special kind of courage is required to perform before an audience. It requires even greater courage to battle one's way to stardom in any of the performing arts. Throughout theatrical history, women have created memorable roles in plays, but not until the early twentieth century were there great women directors. The actresses and dancers will never be forgotten both for their performances and for their many innovations in both the development and teaching of new techniques. The directors Eva Le Gallienne and Margaret Webster have been universally recognized and honored.

Writer Gertrude Stein, whose home in France attracted the greats of literature and art, in this photograph is both the subject and the statue; the sculptor was Jo Davidson.

Maude Adams (1872–1953) contributed more than acting to the theater. She developed new lighting techniques and taught dramatics. At the beginning of the twentieth century she starred in *Peter Pan,* her most famous role.

Ethel Barrymore (1879–1959), who was born in a family of actors, was a star at twenty-two and remained one for more than fifty years. She starred in more than forty Broadway productions.

Helen Hayes (1900–   ) has delighted theater, motion picture, and television audiences for more than fifty years. She has won the highest honors in her profession. Along with Ethel Barrymore, she is one of the few actresses to have a theater named after her.

Numerous black actresses have enriched our theater, films, and television. Ethel Waters, Pearl Bailey, Ruby Dee, and Lena Horne, to name but a few.

Isadora Duncan summed up her contribution to the dance and ballet: "I have only made movements which seem beautiful to me." In the early twentieth century she was a pioneer in modern dance. Her technique of running, walking, and leaping on stage made her dances more meaningful.

Agnes De Mille is a creator of dances, a choreographer. Since World War II, she has worked American folk dances into her ballets, which are frequently woven into plays such as *Oklahoma!*

In the twentieth century, Martha Graham founded a modern dance school, which has had many imitators. She has created 144 ballets, and danced, taught, choreographed, and produced many of the finest modern dance works at home and abroad.

Maria Tallchief, a full-blooded Indian, and Ruth St. Denis made great contributions to American dance.

Actress Ethel Barrymore (above left). Pearl Bailey (above right) starred in an all-black version of the play, "Hello Dolly." The name Martha Graham is perhaps the most famous in modern dance. Below left, she appears as "Herodiade." Below right, American Indian ballerina Maria Tallchief at a special outdoor performance in the nation's capital. Part of the Washington Monument can be seen in the background.

Musicians

America has produced many great singers for the concert halls and opera houses of the world.

Marian Anderson fought prejudice against black performers and was eventually acclaimed in the United States and around the world. Her concert at the Lincoln Memorial in 1939 before 75,000 people and millions in the radio audience, revealed a rich, deep, glorious voice. She began singing at eight years of age in churches, local clubs, and societies. Later she crowned her career as a star of the Metropolitan Opera Company. In 1935 *The New York Times* called her "one of the great singers of our time."

Rosa Ponselle was one of the leading sopranos of the twentieth century. With no previous European training, she was the first American singer to become a Metropolitan prima donna (star). She helped to open the Metropolitan's doors to other young American singers.

Opera stars Leontyne Price and Beverly Sills, Martina Arroyo and Maria Callas are just a few of the women who have received great acclaim in the mid-twentieth century.

Few women have won recognition as composers of classical music or as conductors of symphony orchestras. Many women, however, have made their mark as musicians, composers, and singers of popular music.

Scientists

Women have made outstanding contributions in science. They have been active in medicine and the biological sciences and pioneered in some of the new sciences, such as anthropology.

Florence Sabin (1871–1953) was a graduate of Smith College and a holder of an M.D. degree from Johns Hopkins Medical School. The director of the Rockefeller Institute in 1930 declared that she was "the greatest living scientist." Her specialty was the investigation of the lymphatic system, blood vessels, and red blood cells. She led

Above, Marian Anderson after her 1955 debut at the Metropolitan Opera in Verdi's "Masked Ball." Center, from left: opera stars Leontyne Price, Beverly Sills, Martina Arroyo, and Maria Callas. Folk singer and composer Joan Baez (below) became a hero for her music and her ideals of peace and love.

the movement to redirect the study of medicine away from only the cure of disease to focus more on the maintenance of health.

In the twentieth century Dr. Helen Taussig pioneered in surgical operations on "blue babies"—infants born with a special type of heart disease. Dr. Jane C. Wright, a black physician, was director of cancer chemotherapy and associate dean of New York Medical College.

Lisa Meitner, a German-born physicist, contributed to the development of nuclear research in the area of atomic fission.

Ruth Benedict and Margaret Mead rank among the great anthropologists of the twentieth century. Both have emphasized the role of women in the cultures of the world.

Lillian Moller Gilbreth reared twelve children and also became an engineer and management specialist. She applied scientific management methods to both her home and her business. She was chairman of her department at the Newark College of Engineering and served on numerous government commissions.

Anthropologist Margaret Mead, known for her studies of women and families all over the world, appears before a photograph from her book Family.

10

CAREER BREAKTHROUGHS FOR WOMEN

Less than a hundred years ago, young women were not asked what they planned to do when they left school. A woman's duty in life was to marry and bear children, according to the majority of people—mostly men.

If a woman had to make a living, teaching and nursing were the only respectable occupations. Now, other fields have opened. Medicine, newspaper work, business, engineering, architecture, law, sports, acting, and science are actually welcoming women into their ranks.

Career breakthroughs did not happen overnight. There have always been women who have felt that they had work to do in the world, and that they could not be satisfied until they had done so. For some, it was a very hard fight. Many had to battle for an education or a job. History does not tell about the countless women who were forced to hide their talents and to waste their lives cooking and washing. Today, women are free to perform interesting and exciting jobs. The 1967 Civil Rights Act forbids discrimination in employment on account of sex. As a result of this law, about three thousand charges of "sex discrimination" in employment are brought annually before the Federal Equal Opportunity Commission.

Young women plan to change American politics. Above, students hold an emergency conference at Loyola University in Chicago. Ann Uccello (below left), mayor of Hartford, Connecticut, one of the few women to hold elected political office in the United States. Women are looking to change religious traditions. In 1972, Sally Priesand (below right) became the first woman rabbi in history.

WOMEN IN POLITICS

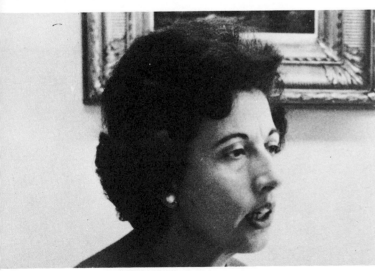

The names listed below are only examples of some of the women who have broken ground in areas formerly reserved only for men. Some already have been discussed.

Anne Royall was a pioneer woman reporter. She came upon President John Quincy Adams (1825–1829) swimming bare in the Potomac River. She seated herself upon his clothes and refused to turn her back until he gave her an interview. After the interview, she allowed him to get out of the water.

Dr. Mary Walker found it necessary to wear men's clothes to assert her right to practice medicine. *Susan B. Anthony* deliberately had herself arrested and fined in order to gain her right to vote. *Elizabeth Blackwell* could not find a landlord who would permit her to hang out her medical degree sign. Dr. Blackwell persevered, however, and helped to establish the New York Women's Medical College in 1866.

Marie Mitchell, an astronomer and educator, discovered a comet by telescope in 1847, becoming the first woman in the world to accomplish this remarkable feat.

Lillian Gilbreth was the foremost woman industrial engineer in the first part of the twentieth century. She combined psychology and industrial research to fit jobs to workers and workers to jobs. As an efficiency expert, she pioneered in scientific management.

St. Frances Cabrini helped to establish sixty-seven orphanages, hospitals, and girls' schools and colleges on three continents. She was the first American declared a saint in the twentieth century, through papal proclamation.

Amelia Earhart was the first woman to fly solo across the Atlantic Ocean in 1932, and the first person—man or woman—to fly across the Pacific Ocean, from Hawaii to the United States mainland. She established both altitude and transcontinental speed records in her day.

Mildred (Babe) Didrikson Zaharias was the foremost all-around athlete in American sports history. In the Olympics of 1932, she won medals for javelin throwing, the hurdle race, and the high jump. She

Dr. Mary Walker (left) wore men's clothing in order to practice medicine. All-around athlete Babe Didrikson Zaharias (right) became the first American-born golfer to win the British women's championship.

won every available golf title from 1940 to 1950. She was outstanding in shotput, figure skating, tennis, billiards, and diving.

Rachel Carson alerted America to the dangers of pollution in the 1960's. In her books *The Sea Around Us* and *Silent Spring* she wrote of the beauty of the environment and how man is destroying both life and his environment.

Margaret Mead has enlightened us about human nature through her writings, her research, and her teachings. She began her studies of girls in Samoa, a primitive society. A leading anthropologist of the twentieth century, she claimed, "I have always done a woman's job, never a man's."

Constance Baker Motley, a black woman lawyer, was a key figure in our nation's campaign for desegregation in the public schools. In 1966, she became a United States District Judge in New York.

Margaret Chase Smith is the first woman to have been elected to serve in both the House of Representatives and the Senate. She is the first woman placed in nomination for the presidency of the United States, at the National Convention of the Republican Party in 1968.

Shirley Chisholm, from Brooklyn, became the first black woman elected to the House of Representatives in 1968. Her work in the fields of education, veterans' rights, and civil rights has been widely acclaimed. In 1972 she campaigned for nomination as the Democratic candidate for president.

Margaret Bourke-White was the most respected woman in the world of photography. Her portraits and picture stories of World War II, of Russia, Japan, China, Turkey, England, Egypt, and the United States have been published in magazines throughout the United States. Numerous books of her photographic stories have been published. She has been named as one of the "top photographer-reporters of the world."

Constance Baker Motley, shown above with President Lyndon B. Johnson, after she became the first black woman selected as a United States District Judge. Outspoken Representative Margaret Chase Smith of Maine (below left) is known for her independence in Congress. In the 1972 Democratic party presidential primaries, Representative Shirley Chisholm of New York (below right) became the first black and the first woman to make a serious attempt at the nomination.

WOMEN AT WORK

In 1970—31.4 million women at work

        38.5 percent of the labor force in United States

Since 1940 the percentage of women

working has nearly doubled.

        Almost 50 percent of mothers

        with children from 6 to 17

        years old are working.

        11.6 million women in clerical work

           Four times the number in 1940.

        6 million women are service workers,

        employed in medical care,

        restaurants, hotels, motels, etc.

           More than three times the number in 1940.

In 1970—4.6 million women in

professional or technical occupations,

or 1 out of every 7 is a woman.

        1.7 million women in teaching;

        69.5 percent of teachers are women

        22,000 women physicians and surgeons

           An increase of 26 percent since 1960.

           7 out of every 100 are women—

           7 percent physicians

           2 percent of dentists are women

        8,000 women lawyers and judges

           Small part of 214,000—2.6 percent

        Less than 1 percent of engineers are women.

In 1970—more than two thirds of

all personnel in banks were women.

        20,000 women bank officers.

        11 percent of all bank executives are women

               United States Bureau of Labor Statistics

In the 1970's women own about three-fourths of the stocks and bonds, 70 percent of the insurance policies, and 65 percent of all savings accounts. They outnumber men by 5 million, yet the control and direction of business and finance remains with men.

WOMEN, WOMEN, EVERYWHERE

Women have even invaded the "sport of kings," as jockeys, grooms, and exercisers for racehorses. They are found among the ranks of the mail carriers, the bus and taxi drivers, and traffic police and state troopers! Women are fast becoming prominent in the field of atomic research and computer mathematics. Throughout all the new technologies of the 1970's, there are, at long last, places for women.

SUMMARY OF

Recommendations of the President's Commission on the Status of Women 1963—First Official Board to Examine the Status of Women in the United States.

- Girls and women should be able to acquire and continue their education.
- Child care services should be available for all families.
- Equal opportunity for women should exist in hiring, training, and promotion in private employment.
- Equal pay should be received for comparable work.
- The provisions of social security and unemployment insurance should be broadened.
- The principle of equality should be extended so that practices of discrimination against women will be ended.
- Women should be encouraged to seek elective and appointive positions in local, state, and national governments.

PROPOSED WOMEN'S EQUALITY AMENDMENT
TO THE UNITED STATES CONSTITUTION

Equality of rights under the law shall not be denied or abridged by the United States or by any state on account of sex.

11

NEW FEMINISM— WHAT WOMEN WANT *NOW*

Judge or factory worker, Cabinet officer or typist, professor or waitress, novelist or technician, voter or non-voter, scientist or mother— women have had to fight their way to personal achievement.

Mere voting rights did not give women equal rights with men. Obtaining the franchise has been only a small part of women's long, hard battle for recognition. The early Suffragists made much of this progress possible. But equality in every field and phase of American life is the goal of American women today. The years of protesting and picketing for better pay, better working conditions, and the right to vote have led to active protests for civil rights, race equality, better housing, day-care centers, peace, and better educational opportunities. In the 1970's some of the leaders are Betty Friedan, Kate Millet, and Gloria Steinem. They call their crusade "Women's Liberation."

Women still seek greater acceptance in the professions. They want the same pay and opportunities for promotion. They feel entitled to and qualified for a proportional share of administrative and executive jobs in both private industry and government. Still, women continue to be restricted by special laws concerned with the type of work they may do, hours, wages, and working conditions. The pattern of inequality still persists. In spite of the federal law of 1963 prohibiting

Above, women employees of Newsweek *magazine charged the publication with discriminatory practices against women in jobs and hiring. The two women on the left are employees of* Newsweek; *next is Eleanor Holmes Norton, New York City Commissioner on Human Rights; and Lucy Howard, legal director of the American Civil Liberties Union. Below, writer Gloria Steinem, an outstanding speaker for the women's liberation movement, founded* Ms., *a new kind of women's magazine, in 1972.*

discrimination in both hiring and pay on the basis of sex, women's salaries are still lower than those of men in the same positions. Prejudice may explain this condition, since there has always been resistance to women as "bosses" over men. And, women are considered to be less career-oriented than men.

What paths are open to women in their search for equality? One is the political route. Women are seeking the passage of an amendment to the Constitution to guarantee equality, in which, however, they would be exempt from compulsory military service. Women have been joined by many men in supporting new legislation to cover such areas as the establishment of child-care centers and equal opportunity for education, and legal rights.

The ballot box is another path. Women seek election as legislators, along with men who will promote women's causes. The courts continue to be used to settle complaints and violations of laws that protect women.

Publicity and propaganda are the techniques of the feminists and women's liberation leaders. They attempt to educate the public and to enlist their support with picketing, conferences and confrontations, meetings, radio, television, books, and magazine and newspaper articles. They use demonstrations, parades, and women's organizations, such as the National Organization of Women (NOW), and women's clubs to promote and publicize their views.

Women's brave deeds and bold thoughts have made our country a better place for life, in this and in generations to come. Women of our time are seeking the fulfillment and satisfaction that comes from a job well done.

Over the years, women have used marches to make their demands known. Above, 1913, below, 1971.

SUGGESTIONS FOR FURTHER READING

Bernard, Jacqueline, *Journey Toward Freedom: The Story of Sojourner Truth*. Grosset & Dunlap, 1964.

Boynick, David, *Women Who Led the Way*. Thomas Y. Crowell, 1959.

Brownmiller, Susan, *Shirley Chisholm*. Doubleday, 1970.

Clymer, Eleanor, and Erlich, Lillian, *Modern American Career Women*. Dodd, Mead, 1959.

DeCrow, Karen, *The Young Woman's Guide to Liberation*. Bobbs-Merrill, 1971.

Friedan, Betty, *Feminine Mystique*. Dell, 1970 (paperback).

Gilfond, Henry, *Heroines of America*. Fleet Press, 1970.

Graff, Polly Anne and Stewart, *Helen Keller: Toward the Light*. Garrard, 1965.

Hole, Judith, and Levine, Ellen, *Rebirth of Feminism*. Quadrangle, 1971.

Johnson, Dorothy M., *Some Went West*. Dodd, Mead, 1965.

Komisar, Lucy, *The New Feminism*. Franklin Watts, 1971.

Lader, Lawrence, and Meltzer, Milton, *Margaret Sanger: Pioneer of Birth Control*. Thomas Y. Crowell, 1969.

Norris, Marianna, *Dona Felisa: Mayor of San Juan*. Dodd, Mead, 1969.

O'Neill, William L., *Everyone Was Brave: The Rise and Fall of Feminism in America*. Quadrangle, 1969.

Ross, Ishbel, *Sons of Adam, Daughters of Eve*. Harper & Row, 1969.

Ross, Nancy W., *Heroines of the Early West*. Random-Landmark, 1960.

Scott, Anne Firor, *Women in American Life: Selected Readings*. Houghton Mifflin, 1970 (paperback).

Shafter, Toby, *Edna St. Vincent Millay*. Messner, 1957.

Smith, Page, *Daughters of the Promised Land*. Little, Brown, 1970 (paperback).

Sterling, Dorothy, *Lucretia Mott*. Doubleday, 1964.

Stevenson, Janet, *Women's Rights* (A First Book). Franklin Watts, 1972.

Stoddard, Hope, *Famous American Women*. Thomas Y. Crowell, 1970.

INDEX

ABOUT
THE AUTHORS

Claire R. Ingraham is a free-lance journalist and educational consultant, who attended Downer College, Lawrence University, for her B.A. and the Pulitzer School of Journalism for graduate work. Appropriately Ms. Ingraham emerges as coauthor of *An Album of Women in American History* after a long career as an editor and ghost-writer. She has also worked in advertising and public relations and has held numerous public-service positions. Ms. Ingraham and her husband, Leonard, live in Fresh Meadows, New York.

Leonard W. Ingraham, Director of Social Studies for the New York City Board of Education, holds a B.S., an M.A., and an Ed.D. degree. Dr. Ingraham has held various fellowships and honors in the educational world. In addition, he has written numerous articles and books. Franklin Watts, Inc., is the publisher of *Slavery in the United States, An Album of Colonial America,* and *An Album of the American Revolution.*